FIRE I

# FIRE IN THE CONSERVATORY

Poems by

Linda Gregerson

Dragon Gate, Inc.

Acknowledgment is due to the editors of the publications in which many of these poems were first published: *Antaeus* ('Goering at Nuremberg' and 'Maudlin; or, The Magdalen's Tears'); *Crazyhorse* ('Much Missed' and 'Beggar-My-Neighbor'); *Field* ('Norway,' 'Rain' and 'Fire in the Conservatory'); *The Iowa Review* ('To Albert Speer' and *'De Arte Honeste Amandi'*); *Ironwood* ('Geometry' [formerly titled 'One More'] and 'A Thursday in November, 5:00 PM'); *New England Review* (*'Ex Machina'*); *Ohio Review* ('Man Sitting in the Sun' and 'Without You'); *Ploughshares* ('Russia, Morocco, Peru'); *Poetry* ('Wife,' 'Frame' and 'The Three-Legged Dog at the Heart of Our Home'); *Poetry Now* ('The Weather,' 'Egress' and 'Neck Verse'); *Shenandoah* ('Alone'); and *The Virginia Quarterly Review* ('Halfe a Yard of Rede Sea'). 'Norway' was included in *Best Poems of 1976* (Borestone Mountain Poetry Awards).

ISBN 0-937872-06-7
    0-937872-07-5 (paperback)
Library of Congress Card Number 82-71648
All rights reserved

9  8  7  6  5  4  3  2
First printing

Published by Dragon Gate, Inc., 508 Lincoln Street, Port Townsend, WA 98368.

# CONTENTS

III

IV

# FIRE IN THE CONSERVATORY

*For Steven*

# MAUDLIN; OR,
# THE MAGDALEN'S TEARS

If faith is a tree that sorrow grows
and women, repentant or not, are swamps,

a man who comes for solace here
will be up to his knees and slow

getting out. A name can turn on anyone.
But say that a woman washes the dust

from a stranger's feet
and sits quite dry-eyed in front

of her mirror at night.
The candle flame moves with her breath, as does

the hand of the painter, who sees in the flame
his chance for virtuosity. She lets him leave

her shoulder bare.
Bedlam's distilled from a Mary too,

St. Mary's of Bethlehem, shelter
for all the afflicted and weak

of mind. The donors conceived of as magi
no doubt. The mad and the newborn

serve equally well for show.
A whore with a heart, the rich

with a conscience, the keepers of language
and hospitals badly embarrassed at times

by their charge. The mirror refuses
the candle, you see. And tears on another's behalf

are not
the mirrors he's pleased to regard.

Who loves his ironies buxom and grave
must hate the foolish water of her eyes.

# CARPHOLOGY

[Gr. καρφολογία (Galen), f. κάρφος twig, straw, bit of wool
+ λέγειν to collect.] The movements of delirious patients, as if
searching for or grasping at imaginary objects, or picking the
bed-clothes; floccilation.


Wool, which gathers, is shorn in a heap,
then gathered and woven and gathered
again. Have you felt how a blanket grows worried
and longs to be cleaned?

Mortality gathers under the nails
and paint them how you will, they tempt
the teeth. The fontanels drip gray
at last, which were last to heal, so nothing

intact but requires some touch
to be still. I finger my days
into little rows; they wouldn't stuff
a pillow. Mornings come round

like so many nosy neighbors, the motes and dust
of consolation. Wax in the ear
and anecdote. When I've picked my mind bare,
I'll go driving again alone

by the side of the bay. The salt there gathers
and blows on the road, the bridge too low
to be seen in advance at all. The lights
come bit by bit.

# EGRESS

Mr. Barnum, Mr. Bailey,
on the other side of the pachyderms, the tank
of fish, there's space for your ruse. Mr. Bailey?

Mr. Barnum. By the palm of your hand
the cleverer. Who culled the word
that conned the people part of the time, in the end

they got what they'd meant to have.
The Siamese twins used to look at the sign
aslant, they couldn't go.

Or had their shortcut built in somehow, while we
need minds like yours. Egress.
Regret. The creature through this door

has a wandering tail. And I, to be here,
have left each other place
as if to return. Fat lady on a poster.

Tom Thumb on a poster. The main event is safely somewhere
off to the left, with the kitchen and the woodstove,
the sugar cookies blistered just enough

to approximate my childhood. The walls
of the exhibition hall are seamless
since you left. We make do

by stepping in fear of a good trap door.

# GEOMETRY

What I like best about the snowplow is morning,
then night, but anyway without the sun.
I drive from town to Old Sixteen and back again, wider.
The sound I make's all mine, like the tunnel from the headlamps,
mine. First I plow with the light and then with the plow.
The best part closes up behind. I could tell you but I won't
how the farms separate, each one packed around a single light
for prowlers or company. The light that's modern and blue
stops farther out and sharper than the yellow kind. I'd as soon
steal a chicken in blue. Where the highway makes a triangle
with Sixteen and County O, a picnic table bellies up.
The tracks fill in. When I wake sometimes
I don't know the room, there's nothing to see by
and nothing to see if I could. The fields
are parceled into squares by roads named for letters
but who could know it in the dark?
Anyone can be here when the night thins out.

## TO ALBERT SPEER

We like the way you look, you see. It's more
what we had in mind. That fellow with his mouth
all to the side and the one
working eyebrow, he makes us feel absurd,

as though our notions were at fault after all.
In a well-appointed room, one's thoughts
are shapely too. But you know! You were a builder
of rooms. Of room. (Forgive me.)

We're learning to read the generals' maps, mysterious
as money: a line may be held, but not in the hand.
There are sliding populations,
so we've had to invent a screen: *Who won*

*the World Series? What's the capital of the state*
*you're from?* The men we took
for figures of speech turn up at our table,
passing the salt, are rather the hosts

than the company. Who knows no history
is also condemned. The macadam leads straight
to the armchairs we've slept in.
Of perfect contrition, a lamp and a shade.

## THE BETTER OF BOTH

The front of his foot so narrow, the hand,
as though everything might escape. He keeps
a file of interesting words and remembers his wife

precisely. The move has partly done him good.
There's a tree, at least, by the window and
a plant inside
that gives him pleasure because of its weight.

Suspension, that is. He watches it hang and divide
the window that frames the tree. The tree and the plant
do not coincide in their seasons. All movement, therefore,

there for him. As Vesalius, he thinks, chose the better
of both, and I have him bound in a book.
Last night, a sound of great anger
or anguish
started up beneath his window. As when

the boy with no legs who frequents your laundromat knows
you think only of him as you change
your dollars and fold your towels and pretend
there's health enough for everyone. So the sound

leaves him stricken, mid-phrase,
at his desk. When the day's poor lymph
begins to leak across his page, It must

have been cats, he decides. He's cold.
And one has chased the other away. And I
neither fed them nor locked one outside by mistake.
He'll open the blinds when the sky's had time
to compose a familiar face.

# NORWAY

Fishbone ground for cleaning, flagstone
halls, girls who wear gray dresses
scrub them blind. It takes a lot of friction,
smoothing stones, your knees grow scales.
When I come back the girls are gone,
my bed is straight and smells of fish.

> This is where she used to work and this
> is where she's buried.

Stone and water stint a farm, grudge
foothold. One white horse,
reluctant pasture. Go high enough,
the rocks aren't even good for hiding.
Tunnels can't be dug and so they're
built, some wooden slats to help
with all that snow and sky.

> And this is what she looked like,
> this is how we knew you right away.

Whalemeat has more blood
than anything that grows on land.
Three days without rain in Bergen
this year: hands hung, mouths hung.
The people get in boats one night
each June and watch the sun
dip down, dip up again. That's festival,
the rest is oilcloth, heavy nets.
In boots like these you only step
on purpose. Winters, no one talks.

> And this is where you'll sleep, we
> haven't used the pillows since she left.

Cloudberries *kjenner du*? the children
pick them, bowls filled up and spilling over.
I've a chair to learn a language in,
the chair's too soft, my memory's wrong,
I rock instead. Outside the grammar's strict,
the square is all right angles, steps,
a fountain blows the pavement wet.
A tall man crosses on his way to class,
he has no family, walks
a line as dazzling as Pythagoras.

       And this, you may not want to wear it,
       is for you to keep.

# A THURSDAY IN NOVEMBER, 5:00 PM

Time after time the sky disengages itself.
Slowly, yes, but the reluctance is your own.
The lawn, the shed for the doves, the trees
hold out in the lack of light
despite the mystery you invent, the walk
you think to take each time you notice dusk.
It's the background shot in Wyoming while the actors
were all indoors. Beneath colors unrelated
to you, of which you never tire, the clouds are steps.
The yard goes blond in patches.
In the time it takes to leave and return
the light has drained, the window become impervious,
you can only see in. It's the face you have to live with.

# ARNOLFINI AND HIS WIFE

There's a bench in front of the very picture
you admire. The room is not obscure, the year
may be judged by the length of your hair and the absence
of an entrance fee. You're alone.
The candle is for Christ
and the dog for fidelity, but no one said how green
her dress. Legibly,
the painter has written his name. In the mirror below,
his face and another's. It's you I cannot see.
Were the lady to pick up her skirts and leave,
would you turn? We are perfectly possessed.

# THE THREE-LEGGED DOG
# AT THE HEART OF OUR HOME

She dances to the wheeze of my lungs. Were she taller,
or had she both hind legs, she would lick my aching knees.
There's nothing like practice I firmly believe. Practice

makes the heart grow fond. When the graft heals,
you've apples on a cherry tree, delicious domestic freaks.

I had a splendid grandmother, I might have made her up.
She wore cotton dresses, usually blue, and glasses
with thin gold frames and plastic cushions for the nose.
The plastic was slightly pink, intended

to blend with the flesh. She never raised her voice.
Her knuckles enlarged, her goiter enlarged.
There are ways within ways. A man will go down
displaying himself in a nursing home. The mystery left,

and there's more than when we began,
has nothing to do with reticence, or safety.

# FIRE IN THE CONSERVATORY

The panes of glass arrived by boat
and sat in boxes for a year,
the man with the mansion in San Jose having died.
The workmen paid from a public collection had never seen

Cape Horn, though one of them loved
the wind through his scaffold, the fog
at its legs, and imagined the moorings might loosen
before they were done. He and the people's Crystal Palace

out to sea, his lunch in its box
attracting an escort of gulls. When the plants moved in,
Mr. Giles of the inspiration at Kew
dispatched a gift: seeds from the Royal Water Lily

sailed with a cargo of hemp through the Golden Gate, as once
down the Nile, up the Thames,
and, musing several seasons away, again
obliged with three-foot leaves. *Royal* for *big*,

or to show whose river counted most,
or because such leaves make the water a pavement
for any man's feet.
The birds of paradise squawked in their bowls.

Observe the plush mouths of dependency. The lily
squandered its blossoming on two
successive nights;
the caretaker's boys lit a road's length

of lanterns, and public officials
launched candles in paper boats: they all moved west.
The fog, remember. The carriage wheels.
The ladies' guild with a plaque. The children

slept for the most part, preferring
the parrot who lived in the central dome, who amused them
by biting the gardener's hose, who rolled a bright eye
and nursed a black tongue.

# GOERING AT NUREMBERG

There are people in my country now
who wait for the rapture in living rooms,
by which they mean
to be gathered whole cloth to the arms

of God. As if to forecast
your later escape, you stood,
eighty pounds less of you stood in the dock
to be judged, your uniform draped like a flag.

What we failed not so much to imagine as
quite flatly to prevent was sponsored
bravado, the one small vial of cyanide burning
a hole through justice, by which

we sometimes mean revenge.
The hangman was left like a bride
forlorn. Malice absconded
and all its voluptuous ballast let slip

within our very walls. You'd colonized
the airier regions for years, had you not?
Wines the poets would envy, art,
as in "he's hung great art

on his walls," and one tubercular
Swedish wife, who suffered *grand mal*
as others among the chosen have suffered
great evil, to serve as a sign.

Like a bank account in some better
South America, this life of the spirit

accumulates. The dashing young flyer
is dashing again, though nearly out of time.

As good for the heart as conscious
election, as good for the profile
as a long silk scarf, the end of hope
is bracing as mountain air. Or so

you'd lead us to believe.
We can see how hope equivocates.
The lost don't send instructions.
Nobody trusts the saved.

# PERPETUAL MOTION

The team knew home was closer across the fields
than around, so Alvin'd come to town, you see,
with the eggs and so forth, and he'd spend it at the Norway

till he fell dead drunk at your feet. That would be
on Saturday. We'd load him in the wagon and he'd
wake up with the sun in his own warm barn. Well this time

they'd plowed in the afternoon, the ground
had froze and the wagon bumped to beat hell.
Beat Alvin's head in any case, the furrows hard

as a woman's heart, till it bumped him out the back
and there he lay. Next morning his toes and his fingers were black.
Oh yes. The old lady was fit to be tied.

What I remember was something else. The years
we'd need no almanac but Alvin's fields alone. And the angle
his herd made, square as a new-hung door, when they reached

the side of the road. Alvin had the light first, behind his parcel
of oak, and Alvin's corn was last to roll
when we hadn't seen rain in a month. Lived with his mother,

drank but once a week. Later we'd keep him company.
You ought to collect, we'd say,
for fallow; you should marry a woman with seven sons,

follow the shade back and forth.
The summer before the war, I'd started inventing.
It ought to have run on water but never came round.

# NECK VERSE

Your father, on the other hand,
was convinced of a stage door to safety

and luck: you knew what to slip the doorman the way
you knew who to touch

for first base seats at Ebbets Field. He broke his back,
but the angle is hard to distinguish from that

which rescued the ersatz priest. Time was,
the right Latin could spare a man's neck. The chosen
walk unseen. The lost . . .

Which leaves you somewhere between the docks
and the deep blue sea, who never trusted either union.

Sundays in August he'd pick out a suit. A regular man
could afford good wool, and the extra pair of pants

came free. The elbows took years to wear out, the pockets
got stained from the chocolate he'd meant for you.

## SMALL MIND

For E.K. Chambers

1

Here's the water no wind finds, so the face
is the one you know.
This muddying cannot be blamed on any disturbance
without. Have you thought
how consolation is wont to congeal?
And here's the friend in the pool, kept there
and likeable by a slightly ironic turn
of the mouth which, sweet coincidence, you
can adjust. No fish worth bait.

2

The circle of trees cannot hurt you,
mirrored thus. The live ones whose likeness
these are put forth
a fine, dusty hope for the future to blight
your lungs, which are also trees,
if branching's the central art.
Lombardy poplar, coast live oak: the list
of reasons is long and breath
is short. The small mind has heard

3

of a larger. A civil servant climbs the steps
to a reading room full of the chosen.
His is the circle beneath a green shade,
while for them, the light sifts down all day.
Who takes his supper alone in a pub between labor
and labor has left us this volume
of community. Now all those books
to be moved to a suburb. Where
will the faithful walk at noon?


4

Pay no attention, the stewardess says,
and you give it the least you can, lest the pocket
enlarge on credibility and the plane
fall down. There's a kind of thinking we call
a flight, and isn't it a perfect lapse?
The way the whales won't come when you watch,
though the ocean does, and will,
whatever
the vacuum that keeps you aloft.

# SHIP

It must be the one we're waiting for,
we the investors, or friends

of the deceased. Our hope's a kind of geography:
each place it lands, a city like ours springs up.

Your daughter's dowry hangs by a bolt of silk
in the hull. Another bolt shortened

to stitch up the corpse. Our gift's
for abstraction: cast money on water

and see what it floats.
White stone steps from the church to the harbor,

as full of intention as interest rates, belie
the long arc back. A blue shoulder held to its task

by men who watch without memory.
Each bright surface coined by the sky is spent

before we can ask our question. One
we'll retire on. With one, we'll get the current right.

# LIKE NEW

The ones too broke or wise to get parts
from a dealer come here where the mud is red
and eternal. Eight front ends

are stacked on girders he salvaged too.
Ask for Bruce, he said on the phone, and doesn't
crack a smile when you show up.
Twenty-four fifty if we find one, sister.

*Bruce*, it says on his coveralls, and *Bruce*
on the ones his helper wears. The routine's so good
they're keeping it. The taillight you can have.

Except for the traffic, the wrong parts of Baltimore
aren't so bad: each house pulling
its straightest face, the curbs and stoops
lined up like a man inverting his pockets

to show he's got nothing to hide. Construction
sites gone aimless and the detours
feeling more like home. You know

where to find a cheap lunch. Up front,
a woman hears the list through twice
before, as to a sweet and original
prompting, she picks fried trout.

Likewise the oyster shucker, pretending
you've asked for a straw with your beer.
He searches the counter above which reigns

a picture of Washington Stokes, retired,
who cleaned fish to order for fifty-nine years.
A girl on a schedule deserves
what she gets, and sometimes gets it kindly, earned

or no. Untouched by heat of sun or city
police, the fair-haired accommodate best
by having everything to learn.

But here comes your beer without a straw,
as though good nature were common as thirst.
Here's Washington Stokes, who would understand
the strategy that lets the fool go free.

# RAIN

You wait and sometimes the gutters fill.
Rust freshens. This is the spider that crawled up the

spout. This is the water that bit her.
A shuttlecock lies in the drainpipe, its feathers drenched.

The set was a gift from friends too old to play.
By now you know the soft parts of the lawn

and the rents in the net. When your sister will,
you play past dark, you can't see the bird

till it drops, perfect weight, on your racket.
Nor can you see her. The sound

might be her breath or her shoes in the grass.
She forgives you, she never stops.

# LINE DRIVE CAUGHT
# BY THE GRACE OF GOD

Half of America doubtless has the whole
of the infield's peculiar heroics by heart,
this one's way with a fractured forearm,
that one with women and off-season brawls,

the ones who are down to business while their owner
goes to the press. You know them already, the quaint
tight pants, the heft
and repose and adroitness of men

who are kept for a while while they age
with the game. It's time
that parses the other fields too,
one time you squander, next time you hoard,

while around the diamond summer runs
its mortal stall, the torso that thickens,
the face that dismantles its uniform.
And sometimes pure felicity, the length

of a player suspended above the dirt
for a wholly deliberate, perfect catch
for nothing, for New York,
for a million dollar contract which is nothing now,

for free, for the body
as it plays its deft decline and countless humbling,
deadly jokes, so the body
may once have flattered our purposes.

A man like you or me but for this moment's
delay and the grace of God. My neighbor

goes hungry when the Yankees lose,
his wife's too unhappy to cook,

but supper's a small enough price to pay,
he'd tell you himself, for odds
that make the weeks go by so personal,
so hand in glove.

# AUBADE

The pool remains clear.
The bedside glass holds water as warm as the room.
It will taste too sweet, the mouth
accounts for that. The light
insinuates, you know nothing of sleep,
you know nothing. If you wait it will dim.
Think of the margin of sky.
Too distant for rain, the fingering clouds.
Good paper before the water and brush.
The sheets are stiff
with expectation. The raveled horizon
comes round again.

# EX MACHINA

When love was a question, the message arrived
in the beak of a wire and plaster bird. The coloratura
was hardly to be believed. For flight,

it took three stagehands: two
on the pulleys and one on the flute. And you
thought fancy rained like grace.

Our fog machine lost in the Parcel Post, we improvised
with smoke. The heroine dies of tuberculosis after all.
Remorse and the raw night air: any plausible tenor

might cough. The passions, I take my clues
from an obvious source, may be less like climatic events
than we conventionalize, though I've heard

of tornadoes that break the second-best glassware
and leave everything else untouched.
There's a finer conviction than seamlessness

elicits: the Greeks knew a god
by the clanking behind his descent.
The heart, poor pump, protests till you'd think

it's rusted past redemption, but
there's tuning in these counterweights,
celebration's assembled voice.

# DE ARTE HONESTE AMANDI

### 1 What Love Is

Fred Kessler, of the East and West of Castro Street
Improvement Club, is willing to roll with the times. For the drought,
he's added Tips to his flyer: Catch the water
that's still too cold, your garden will be green on it.

You want to recycle? For next week's flyer, leave
this rubberband here on your doorknob.
On alternate Sundays for seven years, he's picked up dogshit
from Noe to Church and back again. Don't talk about heart.

You can see what becomes of a neighborhood:
kids half the time, and nobody visibly
off to a job. Curtains like his mother had, the lace
with the squares, for a joke he doesn't quite get.

His mother went to garage sales too. *Save water.*
*Shower with a friend.*
I'm no prude, Fred Kessler says. What kind of people
would put up the sign and the curtains too?

2  Between What Persons Love May Exist

I don't want feelings, his wife said more
than once, especially where family's concerned.
So he didn't say boo when Agnes took the old man's watch.
I'll stick to my own back yard, he thought,

the breeze isn't bad, it's a wonder it gets around.
If he sits with the bottlebrush tree on his right, and the Murphys
aren't back from church, he can look in turn at the full four sides
of wooden stairs, and can nurse an idea he's had. It's the breeze.

I could harness this thing for a job or two, if once
I got the patterns down. And has started to save small pieces of paper,
the blues in a bag, the reds in a bag, for the purpose of experiments
to be devised. Later he'll ask the different tenants to open

or shut their windows in teams. Sunday,
safest to have the Murphys shut. Back to Ireland, he roars
while she cooks, the notion that starts with communion wine
and moves through a lonelier bottle to be slept off. The young ones

swing from the fire escape, pretending to be lost.

3  How Love, When It Has Been Acquired, May Be Kept

That was when the war was on, the one we felt good
to hate, so of course I thought he'd come from there.
It was June. The light grown long again.
She'd roll his chair to the window

and back. But no, you said, it was love.
They were getting it wrong.
A leg. A leg. An arm to the elbow.
Like the man who burned his daughter to get

good winds. The sea for days had been flat
as the sky. He'd walk while the light went down
and could only tell the water from the air by the drag
below his knees. So this is what it's like

to have no body. A perfect benevolent temperature.
The wheels of the chariots grind
in the hulls of the ships. He lay so still he honeycombed,
may he be safe, may we be sound. The time

they bargained for came piece by piece.

4  The Love of Nuns

This one I won't tell you about, since you ought not to know
how it's done. Instead I'll tell you about a way my grandmother had
of closing her mouth, conspicuously, while we displayed the gaps
in our bringing up. Fresh milk made me sick,

for example, and hay made me wheeze. I liked the landscape best
shut down, the white that made a field and a road one thing.
You can't get there from here, but the windows are good
for writing on. Good frost. Good steam. We'd sleep in a bed

that was theirs before, when both of them could make the stairs.
The light had a string that was tied to a post
above my head. If I reached for the light, the cold
came in. You must cover up the children to their chins.

5 Indications That One's Love Has Returned

There's an illness, of the sort that's named for a man
who first imagines that disparate threads might be threads
on a loom, that is called his syndrome, and frightens
the weaver, who cannot unravel by night

what she sees in the day. Their table had the sun for hours.
The piazza was white. They talked
about physicians at home, whose stories were longer, if less
in accord. And about the morning, months ago,

when the color first spread beneath her eyes.
From cheekbone to cheekbone, the smallest vessels had burst
in a pattern called *butterfly*, they'd named that too,
as the tour guides name rocks till you can't see the sandstone plain

anymore, but Witch's Cauldron and Hornet's Nest.
The wings went away. The course of the river that carved the rock
is air now, and baffles intent. She'd been used to a different notion
of course, the kind you might follow for love of the thing,

or of knowledge, the wings in the glass.

# IV

# FRAME

The tree that had patiently framed our view
turned on us once and swelled
with an issue of birds. Each orange breast
too large for its spine, they threatened to drop
and splatter like so many fruits. I'm frightened

of birds in the first place. In Illinois
they stay the right size and only come out by ones
and twos, but I won't go barefoot. Remember
the crack of a wing in the grass? It was warmer
than grass.

I still think the window kept us straight. Twice
a day the light congealed, we could or couldn't
see the bridge for fog. Either way was reassuring.
And if someone had asked, the branch
was too parochial, we knew it

no? making order out of all that sky.
When better dyes arrived in the wagons of entrepreneurs,
the Navajo weavers knew craft and a past
from nostalgia: they began on brighter rugs.
At one point in the border of each, an erratic line

a single thread wide joins the outside
to the pattern at the heart. On a *spirit line*,
does the spirit come in or depart? Our birds
had been eating what the rain turned up,
new rain got rid of the birds. I'm thinking of you.

# BEGGAR-MY-NEIGHBOR

A card game like the one called 'War'


### 1

The change in pitch was explained to me once.
The approaching source

foreshortens the waves, the retreating extends,
and the pivot's the drop you recognize.

If the car goes backward, it's still a drop.
Or the sweet corn planted twice, so less

will be left to the birds. The child
in the house refrains from disturbing

my afternoon nap. I am secretly awake.
Supper by supper, the woman chooses the ripest ears,

boils water, gives thanks that her teeth
are working as well as they do.


### 2

I have alternate plans, should you not
arrive. There are days out here like money.

Creatures as blue as old glass, as the base
of the stemware I've packed away . . .

The tide, I was saying, has left
what I take to be cephalopods. They are blue

with transparent sails.

3

On the bus, a Spanish woman
sits down next to me. Her beard is sparse

and long, and something white, a bit of cream
or spittle, has dried on one of the curls.

*Do you have a quarter? I can't*

*get home.* The hand in her pocket
is next to my thigh, her mind on the stops,

the right one will escape her.
You seem, said the prince,

to know my stops. I don't know how to play, I said.

# THE WEATHER

The women smiled and talked, he stopped listening
before he stopped hearing. What counted for company,
the rattle of a coffeepot, the scatter of gravel
under the Chevy tires, refused to speak up or follow him
somehow. Talk lasted long.
They'd stand too close and make the words slow.
*How are you. Good.* He rolled up cardboard,
put the wide end next to a cream-colored plastic radio.
The White Sox didn't win enough. The weather
didn't change fast enough. He lettered signs
as straight as before and kept the cleanest windows
on the block. Fooled by the glass
or confused by the town, a pheasant broke its neck.

## SIMILE

Hummingbirds go for my eyes, she said,
and was therefore the only one who saw
the juniper's quiet dislodged.
Since most of the world (as a counter-

example) passes me by,
we've hung red syrup outside my room
to sharpen, or alter, the view.
On the one hand, bees; on the other, a cat

too inept to count. The chickadee keeps
trying a version of stationary flight:
batters its head and spills the prize.
Clings to the spout in graceless

reversion. Remarkably improves.
Although I've never seen her eyes go red
from grief or pollen,
the woman may have obscurer means

of subverting propriety. Pale lashes,
as though for sparser defense,
and something in the irises exceeds
their allotted ground. For doggedly

braving anatomy, our bird has nectar
days on end, but not
the corner on accomplishment.
The creature to whom such prodigal

expense of wing
comes easily as breath to you and me
has not been blind
to the strategies of usurpation:

he dives unheralded against
this larger semblance of himself.
To the ear, a plausible engine.
To the competition, cause for retreat.

The victor so efficient at displacing air
turns into it. An empty field.
At one point, the white of her eye
is pierced by brown. This is true.

Around each portal radiates
a lusher brown, since capable of light
and mind. Anomaly
may not appear to see and yet

it has its vividness.
I don't suggest some hummingbird
met with success. The eyes
will spend themselves in causes

less direct. If the jar runs dry,
it's negligence, not scruples.
No error fueled this dialogue.
No fuchsia was the object of desire.

# WIFE

I've had a couple the oblique way,
you know, the one he's not with now,
now he's with me. Both of them were dark,

isn't that funny, and taller than I am.
A voice you'd be pleased to have,
or go home to, though different

on that point, I don't mean to overgeneralize.
Very unique, as my neighbor once said of several
houses in Baltimore. Their voices

were distinct, I'd say. Both good.
The one ran fresh in the middle of words, and clotted
round the consonants. You'd never need dessert.

The other had the tone of hand-rubbed wood,
rows of tasteful bindings. In the head, your own,
something happens to timbre,

like singing in the shower, we're better
for what gets trapped. Spells caution for my vanity,
since I like what I've heard here too,

if the voice is some version of color onstage,
translated by gels,
but not the way the wheel I learned

would lead me to expect. Or the versions
of his memory: the one who was splendid
in front of the fire, the one who got old fast,

the one who could cook.
Can you tell when the reed in the throat
has split? How does the sentence go then?

## ALONE

A silk purse
made out of something equally
unlikely, sweet revenge.
I walked into the castle keep
and stumbled over bones.
I found a moonface, blank as a plate,
and warmed it until I thought its one eye
would open. Here's a muzzle
that won't grow teeth.
And what are you saving my lady my dear?
Why some of what I earn of course.

# MAN SITTING IN THE SUN

His shoulders thin above a slackening breast,
though the man may be thinking of nothing.
He drinks a little lemonade and shades his eyes.
The woman walking toward him must cut through the pattern
cast by a hooped wire fence and before that
cross a street. In one version she is hit by a car.
In another, the heat suffers no interruption.
She reaches the lawn, the peony bush,
the man raises his arm. A fence,
though this one is graceful and in good repair,
won't stop a speeding car.
But for now she knows the ending. The sunlight
taut between the pavement and the eye,
the eye still mobile. If disaster
is deflected except when it strikes
and the record of deflection can be read,
it is neither in her step nor in the angle of his arm.

## WITHOUT YOU

The dinner planned for your arrival has begun.
The snow is less than convincing.
Welcome the spare dry sound of a woman
sweeping her walk. She wears a wool babushka
and a coat with raglan sleeves.
She is not looking pathetic on purpose. You are not
expected to help. On Christmas Eve the men
all go to get somebody out of jail. Sad for the children,
everyone says. The front room is dark except for the tree.
*The cobwebs I can't reach anymore, I can't see either.*
The lacquer on the telephone stand has begun to blister.
An old widower, who forgets,
calls the police. He says she just ran off.

# RUSSIA, MOROCCO, PERU

The man said to me, Did you used to live
in so-and-so, and I answered yes. Across the street,
the opera had just let out. A good cold rain
had stopped. My window faces a part of the sky
that's never red. At either end of the day,
some loosening behind the trees, a little clamor.
If I've come to think, as I still
come home to you, that a tacit sunset's as good as any,
it's not a sign of hope. *We'll go to Morocco, the woman I had*
*was a beauty.* This morning a blue-gray squirrel,
as it moved, lit the yellow grass.
When I wake very early I watch
your face take form, at ease and perfectly opaque.

# MUCH MISSED

### 1

The indiscriminate light comes home
and the sailor comes home from the sea,
who could link his thoughts of her sweet white thigh

to any business at hand. He returns
to blue candles on a chocolate cake, the flickering tokens
of her regard. It's strength of lung

that floats a wish. *The dark one's breasts used to melt*
*when she stretched. Reach me the ashtray, I'd say,*
*and never let on what I watched when she did. Here*

*and gone. She never gave me trouble at night.*
Here's love in a cup,
his Penelope says, May it speed you back
to me.

### 2

Some of this is morning fog and some of it
afternoon. The event somehow escapes her.
City much missed

by landlocked exiles, now
that she's here, she still makes her way by rumor
and the clock. *I can hear the water rising*

*in your sleep*, the separate strands
of raveled breath. Lies down to work,

takes walks in honor of an absent guide.
The tree in the lungs, the bishop pine, these great stiff rattles
protesting the wind.


3

The wind that year blew the topsoil away, and salt
came up the river. Toby came up from town.

Toby with the running eyes and a cane that'd put the fear of God
into any dog
came up from town to be fed, and was, and died

one night when the weather changed.
Not enough breath to cloud the mirror. And later
some woman who came for his shoes. *What did you do?*

We hoped for rain.

# 'HALFE A YARD OF REDE SEA'

Item in the records of the Coventry Cappers,
Corpus Christi pageant, c.1574

An afterthought? When all but one
of the glovers or joiners who signified

Red Sea had been sewn
fine caps for ready

identification? Or was it thriftily
cut in two and hung

on staffs that parted to let God's
people go through? The waters dividing

were not more mute
about their ways and means than this

account book entry made
four hundred years ago. *A wall*

*on the right, a wall on the left.*
We know the hours a man would spend

assembling chamois or lengths of wood
to earn the sixpence that bought

the sea. We know as well as he how white
the hand appears that harms those bent

on harming us.
Gratitude's been brief

as Pharoah's softened heart for longer
than his rue, so books

parcel memory: this I've paid,
this I owe. Though bread lie plentiful

as dew, the people shall measure
the portion they eat, and want

what the past looks like from here
as half a yard of sea might want

the moon. *The wilderness
hath shut them in.* The players in red

are looking the other way. And the mind
must reckon with waters that have no

mind to open or heal so legibly
again.

## A BIOGRAPHICAL NOTE

Linda Gregerson grew up in Illinois, graduated from Oberlin College in 1971, and earned Master's degrees at Northwestern University and The University of Iowa. She is currently completing a Ph.D. at Stanford University.